NERD!VERSE

ARIEL BIRDOFF

FOR MY FELLOW NERDS

CONTENTS

INTRODUCTION

I was first introduced to the magic of poetry in fourth grade by my teacher, Ms. Fegan. Clutching my new *Little Mermaid* notebook, I followed my classmates out into the schoolyard and took my seat on the clover-covered hill. We read some Shel Silverstein, Carl Sandberg, and Jack Prelutsky, along with other classic children's verse and discussed different types of poetry. We were then tasked with writing our own poems over the next few weeks. I filled up my notebook quite quickly, with both rhymed and unrhymed verse about friends, family members, birthday gifts, and woodland animals. Possibly my best poem from that unit (and possibly my best poem ever) was a simple rhyming quatrain entitled "Squirrel's Lunch":

Nip, nip crunch
Nip, nip crunch
This is how a squirrel
eats his lunch.

Brilliant, I know.

Fast forward to my four years at Muhlenberg College, where I studied poetry in greater depth. I had also started reading *Harry Potter*, and was slowly amassing college friends with whom I could gush and commiserate about upcoming books and movies. I was becoming involved with my first fandom.

For several years, my fanaticism was kept to my IRL[1] circle of friends.

---

[1] In Real Life

However, when I started listening to the podcast *PotterCast*, and joined the New York City Harry Potter Meetup, The Group That Shall Not Be Named, I realized that my Harry Potter world was much larger than I originally thought. In 2007, I attended the Phoenix Rising convention in New Orleans with Potter friends from around the world, and thus became a loyal annual con-goer and active fan. One year later, I founded my wizard rock band, Madam Pince and the Librarians. I have fallen so far down the rabbit hole that I've made it my home. It's a Fandom Wonderland. I devoured the entirety of Joss Whedon's repertoire, earned my Nerdfighter badge, got confused about *Battlestar Galactica*, became completely obsessed with every episode of *Doctor Who* ever, fell in love with *Sherlock*, but never strayed too far from my first love, Harry.

Throughout my fandom journey, my notebook and pen have never been far from my grasp. I've been writing poetry, prose, plays, and articles about my favorite books, characters, OTPs[2], and more along the way.

And now, at last, I am sharing with you some of my more whimsical nerdy verse in my first publication.

I hope you enjoy reading NERD!VERSE as much as I enjoyed writing it.

DFTBA[3],

Ariel

[2] One True Paring

[3] Don't Forget To Be Awesome

ARIEL BIRDOFF

ON BOOKS

Journey

I like to read my books on moving trains.
Both flesh and soul depart in haste,
My body travels o'er rough terrain,
Hurtling to a distant place.

Both flesh and soul depart in haste,
A journey far from all I know.
Hurtling to a distant place,
Into the future, or long ago.

A journey far from all I know,
The sway and shake of speeding cars,
Into the future or long ago,
My mind, it soars amongst the stars.

The sway and shake of speeding cars
My body travels o'er rough terrain.
My mind, it soars amongst the stars,
I like to read upon the train.

Public Tears

Each year I read a lot of books
On trains, in planes, in reading nooks.
They make me cry in public space
At times I get some funny looks
As tears are falling from my face. [4]
Perhaps the subway's not the place
To read the epic Hunger Games.
I should wear shades, yes just in case
And hide my sobs lest one exclaim
And call me freak and other names.
I think perhaps it might be smart
To stop my reading on the trains,
But once I open books to start,
I cannot stop else break my heart.

Book Lists

So many books to read, the list is getting long,
I try to read but one per week, and move the list along

---

[4] I made the mistake of reading a good portion of *The Fault in Our Stars* by John Green in a Starbucks. Yeah. That was not a good decision.

ON FANDOMS

Fandom Poetry

For those of you, who do not know,
I am a geek, a dork, a nerd,
Was at a con not long ago
My family thinks I'm absurd.
But you and me? We're kindred souls!
We're happy down our hobbit holes
We write our fics and play our part
We draw fantastic fandom art
But this is what means most to me,
A means of pouring out my heart:
Creating fandom poetry.

I've scripted odes and some rondeaus,
I've very many written words,
A plethora of verse composed
To lots of fandoms I've referred.
At times myself, or in a role,
In Harry's mind I'd take a stroll.
The Doctor always steals my heart
And Panem tears my world apart
With novels, movies, and TV
It wasn't hard for me to start.
Creating fandom poetry.

And if you wish to be a part
Of this lovely nerdy art,
Write a verse or two or three
Cause sharing words will warm your heart
Creating fandom poetry.

Game of Hunger: A Ballade Royale[5]

I sing to you of bloody battles waged
Concerning youths so young and fair and pure,
Of guts and gore all strewn across the page,
A trying story for some to endure.
Though gruesome yes, the tale, it has allure,
A fight to death 'til one remains alive.
Their only purpose now is to survive.

These children starved to death at such young age,
They enter adulthood so premature.
They're forced to act upon a public stage,
So their obedience will be ensured.
The sight of death to which they are inured
Becomes the mother's milk on which they thrive.
Their only purpose now is to survive.

The game is set inside a chargéd cage:
The borders bound and rigged and made secure.
The children's anger spirals into rage,
The slaughtered bodies spread across the moor.
Their liberty is not to be procured!
As twenty-four falls slowly into five,
Their only purpose now is to survive.

To those that watch, their horror's not assuaged:
They're forced to view this massacre impure.
As tributes fall before they come of age,
The viewership begins to be unsure.
Rebellion stirs to find their nation's cure.
United now as one the districts thrive,
Their only purpose now is to survive.

---

[5] See what I did there?

Ode to Vogon Poetry[6]

Oh skittled niggilywit
Thy frundulations are to me
As glarmeled combatchernaughts on a gavish whale.
Broop I beseech thee, my cranting furlingnobs.
And mopeliciously prongle me with wrinkly candlebarples
Or I will smite thee in the scofferbags with my
glarblemuncheon, oh yes I will!

Thursday

This must be Thursday.
Never got the hang of them.
Could be a problem.

---

[6] Odes to Vogon poetry are the fifth worst in the universe. My very own angsty poetry about dying birds written when I had failed a high school Spanish test comes in at number four.

ARIEL BIRDOFF

On Realizing That Robert Pattinson Seems to Have Only One Talent:

Robert Pattinson is hot.
Also is a giant twat.[7]
Only thing he does with ease,
Is jump out of all the trees.[8]

---

[7] Americans pronounce twat so it rhymes with hot.

[8] Seriously. Go check. He does it both in the Harry Potter movies as well as the Twilight movies.

What the Frak?
(This poem is a HUGE *Battlestar Galactica* spoiler. You have been warned.)

I'm almost done with Battlestar—
From series start I've come quite far.
And though I've seen each episode,
My brain feels like it will explode.
I've been quite lost since season three,
Explain this frakking show to me.

So Ellen is the fifth cylon,
Athena's baby, Hera's gone:
Boomer stole her—kissed the chief,
And Colonel Tigh wallows in grief.
D'Anna's back as number three,
Explain this frakking show to me!

Starbuck played the keys with dad,
Adama's always getting mad
Anders's lost inside his head,
Caprica six—her baby's dead.
So before the end of "Daybreak Three,"
For the love of Kobol, will someone please
Explain this FRAKKING show to me!

ARIEL BIRDOFF

The Most Unrequited Love

I spend each night with you, at home entwined,
My fingers trace the contours of your mind.
Your spirit reaches deep inside of me,
It's only you my eyes can ever see.

You've solved the mystery inside my heart.
You've calmed obsession, forced me to restart.
Exploring strange new worlds within my brain,
My need for you could drive a girl insane.

Alas, our love shall ne'er come to exist.
Our lips are cursed: forever gone unkissed.
I'll not be yours; you'll not be ever mine,
My head, my heart, my soul, shall always pine.

To live in love like this, the ache's unthinkable,
But that's the truth, when you are fictional.

Open at the Close

Cloaked in darkness and sheathed with light,
I will brave the harrowing fight.

Into death, I will walk alone.
In the night my patronus shone.

It's come to this. It's coming now.
Your defeat, don't ask me how.

Together, you and I will be
killed at once and so be free.

From this darkness there comes light.
My lion's heart will pierce the night.

And soon you'll see, and fear me, Tom.
I'll reign victorious—and you?

                    you'll be gone.

Puff Pride

I am a Hufflepuff it's true,
One of the proud, one of the few.
You think you got me figured out?
You don't know what you're talking 'bout
So drop that smirk and step on back,
My heart is yellow, soul is black.
You think us quiet and subdued,
A simple folk with love for food?
You think we'd stay out of a fight,
And let some lions take the night?
Well, that ain't how we roll you see
We won't take shit nor bend the knee.
We fought for Hogwarts and we won!
Our loyalty? Second to none.
While others may discriminate
It's hatred we won't tolerate
We'll take you just the way you are
We've got the best approach by far:
We'll warm your heart and feed your soul.
You're welcome in our hobbit hole.
But if you think that we're unfit,
Perhaps you think we lack the grit,
We won't get mad or throw a fit,
'Cause, Hufflepuff don't give a shit.

Meeting Jo Rowling
(October 16, 2012)

Because of you, my life is changed.[9]
With countless strangers I've exchanged,
So many hugs and so much love
So many fan events thereof.
I've traveled far across the states
To many cons on different dates
And now I've thanked you, tête-á-tête
It's been a night I'll ne'er forget.

---

[9] This book is Exhibit A.

Ghostly Walk[10]

As I wandered through the dark,
I heard my name across the park
I looked ahead and there I saw,
A specter floating, soon withdraw.

A scream, it rose up in my throat,
I yanked the collar on my coat,
Then calmed myself with quiet breaths
But soon inhaled the stench of death.

So from that place, I turned and ran
Yet found myself where I began.
Tears sprang hot into my eyes,
My mouth agape with silent cries.

I couldn't take it anymore,
I sank my knees down to the floor
I threw my arms up in the air
"Strike, shadow, if you're truly there!"

And in that moment, suddenly
I woke in bed, quite luckily.
But as relief spread through my frame
I heard the ghostly whisper of my name…

---

[10] Inspired by Leanna Renee Hieber's Magic Most Foul trilogy.

Time and Relative Dimension in Space

The Doctor saves the world most every day
Defeats the daleks, cybermen, and gelth.
He picks companions up along the way
And travels time and space in utmost stealth.

Oh! Would that I was one who'd run away!
I'd grab the TARDIS key and wave goodbye
And with my Doctor I'd forever stay.
Too fast to stop me, should one even try!

A dream like this, a dream it must remain.
For even if the Doctor's tale were true,
Perhaps you think I'm mad, but I'll explain:
I wouldn't leave even if I wanted to.

Yes, even if that famed blue box did suddenly appear,
My friends, my family, and all my loves—are here.[11]

---

[11] OK. Who am I kidding? I would totally go, and then just come back five minutes after I left. You guys wouldn't blame me, right? Right? Guys?

ARIEL BIRDOFF

Elevenses

Ate a salad today for lunch
Even though I'd had a hunch,
That it would actually be more like brunch—
I am really still quite famished.

I ate before the clock struck noon,
Most definitely way too soon.
And now it's early afternoon—
Someone make me a sandwich. [12]

---

[12] (Witch.)

An Offer She Couldn't Refuse
for Carol and Tom Cronin

A tale of love about Mr. and Mrs.
About how Mr. Tom Cronin came to choose
His lady Carol. She surpassed his wishes,
So gave her an offer she couldn't refuse.
A marriage took place, it was sealed with kisses
They vowed their hearts to each other they would fuse.
And stay as one 'til they slept with the fishes.
For now and forever, she'd remain his muse.

A Sicilian tale of love so glamorous,
A love so deep they'd never want to lose.
If in danger, they'd go to the mattresses
And hope the situation would quickly defuse.
Despite the risk of possible damages,
Together the pair will fight their way through.
Their union is one to trump all marriages,
Since he gave her an offer she couldn't refuse.

The Winter Knight
for Miles Remite

The snowy landscape stretched ahead
Before the Winter Knight.
A dangerous adventure
With wildlings and wights!
The brave young knight gave up a cry,
"I'll find your secrets yet!
"Onward, great North, no matter the cost,
"I'll give my blood and sweat!"
The Winter Knight rode fast and true
And faced so many trials
But luck for him and for his house,
The Winter Knight was Miles.

Good Miles rode up through the wood
The snow kicked up behind.
His thund'ring mare picked up speed,
The fastest of her kind.
On a quest for his Lord Bran,
Young Miles did embark
Perchance to find out threats in snow
Or evil in the dark.
But what he wished and hoped to find
Way up in the unending North
Discovery of lands unknown,
So that his house may venture forth.

The House of Stark, both tough and strong,
Sat high in Westeros,
Quiet, regal, stoic and proud,
Though never grandiose.
Below the wall, the family stayed,
Until a plan was born:
When Miles Stark had come of age,
His loyalty was sworn.
"Off to explore, I freely go,
"Off into cold, and into dark,
"I ride beneath the direwolf
"Of my family home: House Stark!"

Good Miles traveled far and wide
In the world beyond the wall.
On his return, he told his tales
Of all that did befall.
Much glory did that Miles bring
To his Lord and to his house.
Though in time he moved away
And settled further South.
Yet far away from his home,
In weather warm and bright,
Young Miles' heart remained a Stark
And always was the Winter Knight.

ARIEL BIRDOFF

ON WRITING

Penergy

I call myself a wordlebug
I love to make shit up.
Sometimes I'm like a languathug
My words will fuck you up.
I guess I am a poe-geek
So nerdy in my verse.
'Though some might call me poe-freak
I guess it could be worse.
I've tried to write proformally,
In favor of the norm,
While others rhyme miltonicly,
I've never liked his form. [13]
It's much more fun to termerate
Than use existing words.
I'll use them when I conversate
Along with other nerds.
My love of language smithery
Is part of who I am.
I'm full of wild penergy
And I don't give a damn.

---

[13] Technically this is a lie, but Len Roberts told me it's OK to lie. I do feel the need to confess though. I am actually quite a big fan of Milton's work; I just liked the way the line flowed.

ARIEL BIRDOFF

AUTHOR'S NOTE

Many of the poems in this book are written in or loosely based on specific verse forms.

1. *Journey* (pantoum) – A pantoum usually consists of four quatrains with a strict structure of repetitive lines. The second and fourth lines of each quatrain are repeated as the first and third lines of the following quatrain. This continues until the last quatrain where the first and third lines of this stanza are the second and fourth of the penultimate. The third line from the first quatrain is the second of the final, and the first line of the poem is the repeated as the last. A pantoum can be quite confusing.

2. *Public Tears* (Malaysian sonnet) – Similar to an English sonnet, a Malaysian sonnet uses a rhyme scheme of aababbcbccdcdd.

3. *Book Lists* (Poulter's measure) – Made up of only two lines, a Poulter's measure's first line is in iambic hexameter and split evenly by a caesura (break). The second line is written in septameter with a caesura after the eighth syllable.

4. *Fandom Poetry* (chant royal) – Consisting of 3 eleven-line stanzas followed by a five-line envoi, the chant royal's stanzas rhyme ababccddedE, and the envoi rhymes ddedE.

5. *A Game of Hunger: A Ballade Royale* (ballade royale) – Usually written in iambic pentameter, the ballade royale is comprised of four seven-line stanzas with a rhyme scheme of ababbcC.

6. *Ode to Vogon Poetry* – This piece does not employ a specific verse form, but is rather a mimic of Vogon poetry. Vogon poetry, according to Douglas Adams's *Hitchhiker's Guide to the Galaxy*, is the third worst in the universe. As stated in an earlier footnote, Odes to Vogon Poetry are only the

fifth worst.

7. *Thursday* (senryu) – A senryu is a three-line poem similar to the haiku. While the syllable count of 5-7-5 remains the same, a senryu is usually a humorous poem that is not about seasons, but rather about human nature.

8. *On Realizing that Robert Pattinson Seems To Only Have One Talent* (chastushka) –. A chastushka is a traditional Russian folk song with a four-line verse and an abab, abcb, or aabb rhyme scheme. It is usually humorous.

9. *What the Frak?* (stave stanza) – This poem is only loosely based on a stave stanza. A stave stanza is usually written in tetrameter where the last line of the first six-line stanza is a refrain for subsequent stanzas.

10. *The Most Unrequited Love* (sonnet) – This piece is based on a basic sonnet with an aabbccddeeffgg rhyme scheme.

11. *Open at the Close* – While this poem uses a strict rhyme scheme (aabbcc...) and layout (six couplets), it is not based on any specific verse form.

12. *'Puff Pride* – This one is also not based on a specific verse form, but rather is written in a specific meter. Iambic tetrameter is a line consisting of four iambic feet.

13. *Meeting Jo Rowling* (octave) – An octave is a one-stanza poem with eight lines. While any meter is appropriate, it should stay the same throughout. This one is written in iambic tetrameter.

14. *Ghostly Walk* (gothic verse) – This type of poem does not require any specific form; it is only the macabre subject matter makes it what it is.

15. *Time and Relative Dimension in Space* (sonnet) – This poem is inspired by the basic sonnet with an ababcdcdefefdd rhyme scheme.

16. *Elevenses* (rhupunt) – This poem is loosely based on a

rhupunt. A rhupunt consists of several three to five line stanzas with four-syllable lines (I disregard the four-syllables-per-line requirement. The rhyme scheme is aaabcccb.

17. *Penergy* – This one is not based on any specific verse form. It is a one-stanza poem with a rhyme scheme of ababcdcd etc. and alternating tetrameter and trimeter lines.

18. *An Offer She Couldn't Refuse* (Sicilian octave) – A Sicilian octave is an eight line poem with eleven syllable lines called hendecasyllables. It has a rhyme scheme of abababab. This poem is made up of two Sicilian octaves.

19. *The Winter Knight* – This poem is written in the style of the George R.R. Martin character, Marillion the Bard, based on his song about King Robert. Marillion's work unfortunately lead to the removal of his tongue. I hope to be more fortunate.

ARIEL BIRDOFF

ACKNOWLEDGEMENTS

Deepest thanks to everyone who has helped this book come into existence. Thank you to my beta readers Kelly Zepha Owen, M.E. Lerman, and Lee Seigel. You guys are so fetch! And of course, four candy canes for my editor, Karen Halpenny. You go, Glen Coco!

Indiegogo.com wins the Internet for being the medium through which I was able to crowd-source the funds for this project. And of course, one hundred house points each to all of my backers! Most notably Michael Bekman, Brian Remite, Stacy Pisani, Adam Hedges, Susan Stone, Tom Gavin, Alisa and Daniel Boudon, Miranda Koss, Carol and Tom Cronin, and Phillip Levsky.

So much appreciation to my wonderful fandom friends and family, especially those who have been responsible for organizing conventions, Meet Ups, podcasts, fan sites, and Wizard Rock festivals. You have enriched my life immeasurably. Thank you so much for your friendship and support. You are at least 20% cooler.

The Star of Kahless goes to every writer (book, TV, or otherwise) who has created a magical universe for me to explore. Obviously, this poetry could not have happened if it was not for all of you.

A tip of my very cunning hat to every English/Writing teacher I have ever had. I think I may be just about the luckiest student in the world to have had such exceptional teachers since the fourth grade. It's no wonder I can never seem to stop surrounding myself with literature.

Thank you also to my parents and my grandmother who have always supported and encouraged me whenever I began a new project or endeavor. Even though this whole nerd poetry thing might still confuse them, their support never wavered.

Lastly, Adam, you are the Han to my Leia. You have been my favorite beta reader and editor from the start. Despite all of my rough drafts, you still think of me as a talented writer. You had me at Doctor Who.

ARIEL BIRDOFF

ABOUT THE AUTHOR

Ariel Birdoff was born in New York City some time ago. After attending college in Pennsylvania, she moved back to New York City and now lives with her boyfriend and a lot of books. She is a compulsive crafter, obsessive YA reader, and enormously enthusiastic librarian. This is her first book. You can find her on the Interwebs at http://nerdywordythirty.blogspot.com and follow her on Twitter: @Madam_Pince.

www.ingramcontent.com/pod-product-compliance
Lightning Source LLC
Chambersburg PA
CBHW051741040426
42447CB00008B/1250